Juniors & Middlers

How to get Middlers and
Juniors grappling with
big truths about God,
by involving them and
building relationships
with them.

Joyce Gibson
&
Eleanor Hance

 VICTOR

BOOKS a division of SP Publications, Inc.
WHEATON. ILLINOIS 60187

Offices also in
Whitby, Ontario, Canada
Amersham-on-the-Hill, Bucks, England

JOYCE GIBSON, senior editor of Scripture Press Middler/Junior materials, has led juniors in Sunday Schools, youth groups, junior churches, and Vacation Bible Schools for 26 years. She is currently working with 4th-, 5th-, and 6th-graders. Joyce leads workshops across America and Canada.

ELEANOR HANCE former director of the Department of Christian Education at Barrington College, R.I., has for many years been working with juniors as Child Evangelism director, curriculum writer, and teacher. She has contributed chapters for two books: *Youth and the Church* by Roy Irving and Roy Zuck, and *Childhood Education in the Church* by Roy Zuck and Robert Clark.

Third printing, 1984

Bible quotations are from the King James Version unless otherwise noted. Other quotations are from the *New International Version* (NIV) © 1978. The New York International Bible Society. Used by permission.

ISBN: 0-88207-145-9

VICTOR BOOKS
A division of SP Publications, Inc.
Wheaton, Illinois 60187

Contents

Preface

Jesus, a teacher who used many before-his-time methods, commanded His followers to go and teach. We who teach God's Word to Middlers and Juniors readily acknowledge that He promised the power we need for our teaching. But have we noted that throughout the Gospel accounts He also provided procedures for effective teaching? We can teach God's Word effectively to boys and girls when we use His key of arousing their want-to.

It always arouses our own want-to when we see what happens after a student is aroused! That's how we felt as we talked with boys and girls and their Sunday School teachers across the country.

We met teachers who are allowing God to control their life priorities, who are making time for thorough lesson preparation, who are second-mile teachers, praying daily for their pupils and finding time for them outside class.

We heard how Middlers and Juniors respond when a teacher builds a personal relationship with them. We saw how pupils master Bible information when it is conveyed with sparkle, when it is visualized, and when recall is frequent and fun. We saw how students were making discoveries in God's Word and grappling with big truths when their teachers got them involved. And how we rejoiced to see lives changed when children were led to respond to the Lord in loving trust and obedience!

You too can see Middlers and Juniors want to learn God's Word and respond to Jesus Christ as Saviour and Lord. We pray that this book will help you.

1
Seeing Juniors and Middlers as They Are

"Hand-wavers and I-knowers!" That's how one educator described pupils in grades 3 through 6, expressing his delight in their enthusiastic response to his teaching. "Insatiable learners," says another educator about his "turned-on kids."

Sunday School teachers in London, Ontario described their youngsters as "inquisitive, spontaneous in expressing excitement over Bible truths, both serious and practical in their zeal for applying those truths to life."

Sounds ideal. You'd expect a waiting list of teachers wanting a chance to work with preadolescents. But not so! At least not so in most churches. Why? These same children can drive these same teachers to distraction.

"They're so boisterous some weeks I can hardly make them listen to anything I say!" one teacher complained.

Who are these children who are both the delight and despair of adults? Why are they sometimes "noisy" and "impossible"? Are the years between grades 3 and 6 something to get over as quickly as possible, somewhat like an embarrassing case of hiccups? Wonderfully, the hand that formed 8 to 11-year-olds also provides the key for working with them successfully.

It helps to remember that we all were born with built-in growth timetables. Following God's schedule of growth is an important part of God's plan. At each stage of development children have a built-in readiness physically, mentally, and emotionally to learn and respond

in ways that please Him. The Middler and Junior years abound with priceless opportunities to lead boys and girls into Bible truths they are now ready to receive. These are the years for introducing children to Jesus Christ as Saviour and helping them express their love for Him in ways that are unique to their stage of development.

Let's look briefly, then, at general characteristics of children in grades 3-6 to discover how best to work with them. But first, a couple of definitions. Middlers are boys and girls in grades 3 and 4. Juniors may or may not include children in grade 4 with those in grades 5 and 6.

It's an expansive age

By grade 3 children are emerging from the cocoon of their home environment and stretching their wings with a curious look at the outside world. Many today are experiencing things we adults only read or dreamed about when we were their age. Opportunities abound for delving into science, photography, music, sports. Families travel and entertain guests who captivate children with accounts of trips abroad. The library buzzes with hungry readers checking out books on almost every imaginable subject. On television children observe news as it happens. They flit from desert to ocean to moon and back again almost as fast as they can blink. In our shrinking world, experience—or at least vicarious experience—is just a flip of the wrist away.

It's an expansive age socially too. By grade 3 children are joining every available group and forming clubs on their own. They have friends over or go to a friend's house to reorganize a hobby collection, to work seriously on a model, or to "just jabber."

Tuned in to what's happening in the teen world, many of the more mature Juniors are on tiptoe with eagerness to experience what makes life fun for teens. They envy what appear to be the delicious freedoms of adolescence. They copy their language, ape their gestures, listen to their music, and then suddenly bounce back to their own freewheeling world again, glad to postpone the load of responsibility their teen heroes have to assume.

These years are the vital ones for missionary education, for acquainting our students with a panorama of Bible history, for tracing God's plan of redemption through Scripture, for building understanding of the church and a Christian's relationship to it, for developing their understanding of who God is and how He works on our planet, and for experiencing the nearness of God and the quiet wonder of genuine worship.

It's an action age

Just for fun, read the next sentence aloud as fast as you can. Middlers and Juniors [*take a deep breath*] run, slide, push, pull, skid, leap, hurl, twirl, spring, sprint, yell, yank, wiggle, giggle, bolt, blurt, climb, crawl, slam, bang, whoop, and holler.

Yes, these are our students. Almost any combination of action and sound tells their story, for they are on the move and usually in a hurry with plenty to talk about as they go. Adventuresome, agile, bent on achieving, they are eager to try things out for themselves. However, zest and productivity evaporate when these same children are called from a self-directed activity to do an ordinary chore. They will dawdle, moan, and groan, and appear completely incapable of even superficial work!

This is not the age for dull lectures or boring, useless tasks. The key to teaching turns smoothly when a teacher discovers how to harness their energies in activities that are both practical and meaningful. This is especially true when the children themselves have had an opportunity to plan at least part of the learning task and when they see that what they learn can make a significant difference in their lives *now*.

It's a thinking age

"Is it true?" "Does it work?" "How do you know?" Our concrete-thinking Middlers investigate whatever sparks their interest—and almost everything has potential for being picked up by their far-reaching antennae. They are stretching out with questions and exclamations as they observe people, places, and things.

Juniors probe facts of natural science, experimenting to see what works. They pack away information, memorizing facts and figures by the yards. But they are getting ready for more abstract thinking. They are beginning to evaluate social issues, holding up black and white yardsticks and announcing their judgments. They pose serious questions to parents and teachers, expecting them to point out authoritative answers which they can search out for themselves.

They're full of curiosity and exhibit boundless energy when pursuing something that interests them, impatiently brushing aside anything that seems unrelated or too vague to grapple with.

These are the skill-building years in which older Juniors tool up for serious academic study. Teachers at school are stressing how to track down information in a library, organize research, work independently, and be able to hand in assignments on time.

These are the skill-building years at Sunday School too, in which Middlers and Juniors learn their way around God's 66-book library, the Bible. These children are ready for learning to look up references, reading verses for meaning, memorizing key passages, and developing the habit of daily Bible reading for their personal spiritual nourishment. Under your guidance in class they can search the Scriptures to look squarely at life issues from God's point of view and think through the implications of practical obedience.

It's an expressive age

With one hand these children reach out to take in. With the other they reach in to give out. They are amazingly adept at talking even while listening, a feat most adults can't handle! Theirs is a speak-up age. They are usually frank with one another and with adults. Rather than comply silently with authoritarian directives, they are prone to question, "Do I have to do it that way?" They thrive in an atmosphere in which they can discuss, set their own rules, plan projects, and evaluate their own progress.

They can express their ideas in stories, skits, art, and music. They design newspapers, organize groups, prepare reports, debate issues, record polished dialogues on cassette. The restless movement of their hands and feet indicates their craving to be busy doing something— writing, drawing, painting, running, helping.

They have bubbling springs of creativity, though in some cases these may be undercover. More and more of life's experiences are coming prepackaged so that our students are being denied the challenge of starting many things from scratch. What a privilege to be

God's instrument to unclog barriers and stimulate creativity so that our students can express themselves for God's glory!

It's a responsive age

It's a chain reaction. When you set in motion physical exuberance, mental alertness, social gregariousness, and readiness to develop ideas—it's certain to produce a responsive learner. Where else do you get everyone in a group volunteering for a job before they know what the assignment is? In what other department of the Sunday School do you have pupils arriving early for a service project—an *hour* early, "just in case you need me for something"?

But Middlers and Juniors are responsive in other even more important areas. They are responsive to God's truth when they see how it applies to their here-and-now living. And they are responsive to God's Son when He is lifted up as their Saviour and Lord.

This is where you come in, if you have been called by God to teach Middlers or Juniors. You'll find them responding to you—to Christ in you. As you look to the Master Teacher for the insights and resources you need He will use you to turn on their learning want-to. He will use you to guide these responsive youngsters to opportunities in and out of class to test the reality of the spiritual truths they are learning with such facility.

What excites third-through-sixth-graders to learn about God's Word and about being related to Him personally? The key is motivation. "It's easy to learn when I feel like learning," your student tells you. "I learn best, not when I have to learn but when I want to!"

Thinking it through

1. What are Middlers and Juniors like? List as many of their characteristics as you can. Then review the chapter.

2. Which characteristics do you enjoy most? Which cause you the most problems? Is your attitude toward teaching Middlers or Juniors positive or negative?

3. What opportunities for ministry will come to you as a teacher of Middlers or Juniors because of their unique characteristics?

2
Becoming a Second-Mile Teacher

What teacher hasn't dreamed of eager students, absorbed students, all-fired-up students? Who among us hasn't wished students came because they didn't want to stay away, and stayed and stayed because they didn't want to leave? Who hasn't prayed for responsive students, converted students, committed students?

But what do we sometimes get? Students who sprawl and thump, scowl and doodle, shrug their "I-don't-knows," and make a big deal over a crawling bug. When the bell rings, they almost fall on their faces getting out of class.

Want-to is an odd thing. You can't demand it. You have to woo it and draw it out. It's down inside each child. Each has that basic human craving to know, to get answers to his questions. But his want-to must be turned on! This cultivating of want-to has to do with both the person you are and the way you teach.

What is your confidence rating?
Not how confident are you that you can teach (that's important), but how much confidence do your students place in you?

Jesus' class, the Twelve, had complete confidence in Him: "Lord, to whom shall we go? You have the words of eternal life. We believe and know that You are the Holy One of God" (John 6:68-69, NIV). Peter's affirmation says, "We want to learn from You, Teacher, because we have confidence in You." What makes for this kind of confidence?

11

Knowing God's Word Nothing produces a ho-hum class faster than a teacher who either doesn't know what the Bible says or gets the facts confused: "Hmmm, well, I've forgotten the name of this guy who was talking to the prophet, but he wasn't important anyway. Oh, wait, I didn't tell you something that happened..." Of course, once in a while you may flub. Who's perfect? But it will be the exception, not the rule. People were always astonished at Jesus' teaching because He taught "as one having authority and not as the scribes" (Matt. 7:29). He knew what He was talking about.

Teaching with conviction Conviction is something more than head knowledge—it's heart assurance. You've got to be so convinced of what you are teaching that it comes from "the abundance of the heart" (Matt. 12:34). A teacher in Westfield, Massachusetts says, "I never teach a lesson unless I have received some personal truth for myself or some new insight from the Word that I never saw before. I then have a truthful enthusiasm that is fresh in presenting the lesson." Jesus often expressed conviction: "Ye have heard it said ... but I say unto you ..." (Matt. 5:21-22, 27-28, 33-34).

Willing to answer questions That doesn't say you always know the answer, but you are willing to answer. Jesus never put down a questioner by ignoring him or telling him not to interrupt. You may not answer at the point the question is asked, but you will at least come back to it at an appropriate time. You won't lose face if you admit you don't know. Children like honesty. You can keep their confidence if you tackle the job of finding the answer together.

Coping with problems Do you have class cutups or detractors? Jesus knew what it was to have people try to upset Him. We marvel at His wise responses. Oh, to be so perceptive and courageous! You can be—the Lord lives in you. Does it amaze you that you, if you're a Spirit-led teacher, have an ability in teaching which a secular teacher can never realize no matter how much he hones his educational skills? Some Junior boys, for example, like to be magicians, pulling out of hidden places snakes, toads, bugs, and other goodies. Now obviously you don't have to pet snakes to be a second-mile teacher. But if you react to harmless "shockers" with good nature and interest, you will gain stature.

Purposeful, posed, pleasant In that order, too. Jesus knew what

He was about so there was no need to be harried, pressured, or rushed. Purposefulness produces poise and poise produces assurance. And that good feeling of being on top of things makes you feel and act pleasantly.

Someone to count on There are quite a few ways your class should be able to count on you—count on you to be on time (except in an emergency); count on you to have materials on hand and in order; count on you to keep promises and confidences; count on you to be on their side. Children may not comment on the sharp pencils or the clean chalktray or the neat cupboard or the changed bulletin board, but details add up to an overall impression of a dependable teacher.

How's your rapport?

Rapport? That's sympathetic relationship, a drawing together. You don't have to win a popularity poll or beauty contest or athlete-of-the-year award to attract Middlers and Juniors. Rapport is established by something deeper. There's something about the way you come across, about the way you handle things, and about what you do for the needs of individuals.

Did Jesus have rapport? He spent time with the Twelve, hiking, eating, listening, talking, entering into their activities, showing them by His actions, caring and helping. Helping—He helped fishermen fish succesfully; He helped Peter with his ill mother-in-law; He helped Peter overcome guilt. He helped Peter. . . . He was always helping Peter! Do you have a boy like Peter?

Spend time together A teacher in Sarasota, Florida had a boy who reminded her of Peter. He monopolized with interruptions, spitballs, mimicking, and vocal demonstrations against serious Bible study. It was a constant battle to see which of them would lead the class. Trying to get next to him, the teacher began a Saturday-of-the-month class activity. They hunted fossil shark teeth. They swam. They went fishing. This second-mile teacher doesn't fish, but became something of a heroine by untangling a biting, kicking seagull from a line. And Peter? His mother said he had never before related to any teacher. It was a beginning to at least be getting a hearing.

Study together A teacher in Roslyn, Pennsylvania takes her

girls home to lunch on Sundays to work on their Student Manuals together. It's a comfortable time for talk. Other teachers plan a catch-up evening, including some fun and refreshments with study.

Keep in touch   Many teachers send personal notes on Sunday School papers to absentees, telephone each pupil during the week, and make home visits. A teacher in Agawam, Massachusetts realizes her pupils are whole persons with multifaceted needs. She writes: "When I introduce myself to new 5th-graders, I put my name and phone number on the board for them to copy. Then I tell them I am available to them at any time they need me, or if they just want to talk to someone. I have received some calls, but mostly to talk about our lesson. One time a girl called when her mother went to the hospital and in following this up, her mother received Christ. That was great!"

This teacher also visits homes at least twice a year, and sometimes more, so that parents will know him better since most are not church people. He calls on the phone as often as possible to make his Juniors feel he is their friend. This has reduced discipline problems.

Talk together   Some teachers feel they don't do well with the talk approach. Children communicate with their peers, but clam up when a teacher asks, "Did you have a good week?" Wrong question. It's hard to recall. It doesn't really lead anywhere. Try a question or comment about a favorite activity—sports, television, motorcycles, a local event. Look around. Pam is skinned and scraped. She *wants* to talk about her bike accident.

Work together   Never do for Middlers or Juniors what they themselves can do. Make a list of jobs. Assign pupils to as many job-of-the-week or job-of-the-month positions as you can create. One department met on the all-church work day to repair their song-books. They plan to go on to repainting furniture.

Share experiences   A teacher in Mishawaka, Indiana reports they have 5 to 8 learning centers for early-comers among their 56 eager learners. What an opportunity for getting to know each other! When pupils get to know you, they will open up on things that bug them, fears, friends, and questions on spiritual matters.

Make decisions together   Teachers are authority figures, but there is a difference between being an authority on God's Word and authoritarian in power. Some decision-making can be shared. Older

Juniors especially like to be asked their opinions. And they have worthwhile ideas, even about such important subjects as class behavior.

Meet needs Everyone has basic human needs for acceptance, belongingness, recognition, and security. Strong bonds are forged when a teacher contributes toward filling these needs. Tom's aggressive behavior was a cry for help. "I'm somebody—please notice me!" He was noticed all right—as a disrupter of stories, a usurper of time, and destroyer of organized programs. More than once Tom asked the Lord to help him, and we can be sure his prayer was answered. But for change of behavior the Lord chose to work through teachers. The breakthrough came when Tom was asked to be Stephen of Acts in a program. "Not Tom!" said wise teachers. "He'll cut up and ruin the program." But we did it and Tom did it. He had been given responsibility and he came through. He had been recognized. He could do it again.

Are you a second-miler?

Finish this statement: "I remember a teacher who. . . ." Nine times out of ten it will be a second-miler, a wholehearted teacher. When was Jesus a second-miler? All the time. He taught every "class" in an eager, selfless, uncomplaining all-out way. He never did anything halfheartedly. Look at the energy with which He demonstrated righteous anger by clearing the temple. He taught and healed so strenuously that one day He fell asleep in the fishing boat. He prayed most of one night and then walked on the stormy water to rescue His students.

Then look how He led students on a climb up Transfiguration Mountain. Wasn't there an easier way to tell them He would die and come alive? He chose the most impressive means of teaching, regardless of time and effort.

What is there about a second-mile teacher that helps juniors want to learn? It's that extra effort which captures attention and impresses deeply by communicating worth and meaning.

Here are some second-milers:

• The teacher who always brings in current news and pictures to relate the Bible to now such as a search for Noah's ark, a flood to compare with Noah's experience, information on whales, what's happening in Israel to fulfill prophecy, interesting science facts to prove biblical creation.

• A teacher who takes his class to see how a potter works clay into a vessel, and to a synagogue to hear about Passover observance today.

• A teacher who makes a model of a brazen serpent (junkyard material) and a Palestinian house out of real stones.

To sum up, a second-miler is a teacher who does all the pluses because he believes this is part of the Lord's way to make Bible truth meaningful and impressive.

Middlers and Juniors need the security of a teacher in whom they can place confidence. They need to sense belongingness, recognition, and approval in a drawing together with teacher and class in a sympathetic relationship of good rapport and esprit de corps.

They need the feeling of achievement in successful learning which starts out with a hunger-need for something personally meaningful and is nurtured by the selfless second-mile teacher who goes all out to impress God's Word deeply on human hearts.

Thinking it through

1. How can you help students have enough confidence in you to want to learn from you?

2. What is rapport? Make a checklist of ways to develop rapport. Then evaluate yourself.

3. Get together with another teacher and compare successful ways you have used to stir up interest at the beginning of class.

4. What do the authors mean by being a "second-mile" teacher? Why does second-mile teaching help Middlers and Juniors want to learn?

3
Exploring
the Teaching Process

"I can't get Melissa to do anything in the kitchen," a mother complained. "She has absolutely no interest in cooking. All she wants to do there is make snacks and leave a trail of crumbs, dirty dishes, and an open peanut butter jar."

But things changed suddenly for Melissa. A friend was coming for dinner, and Melissa asked her mother to serve the family's favorite menu. Mother saw an opportunity that she could not resist.

"Oh, we would all enjoy that," she told Melissa. "But I don't see how I can serve it. I just don't have time to fix such an elaborate meal. A casserole would be much quicker."

"Oh, please let me make dinner," Melissa begged. "I know I can do it if only you'll show me how!"

• • •

Though she didn't realize it, Melissa's mother used a teaching process that has been proving effective in Sunday School. Her mother was using an approach to teaching that is called Guided Discovery Learning.

Simply put, this approach involves the learner as directly as possible in the learning process. He learns best when he personally desires to find out what he needs to know in order to be able to do what he wants to do. In Sunday School it means arousing the want-to so that the learner makes it his job to discover from the Word of God lesson truths and their implications for him personally.

Guided Discovery Learning is woven throughout each lesson in the curriculum. It is summed up neatly in three words found in every lesson: Focus, Discover, Respond. Let's see what these words mean for the children in your class.

FOCUS: capturing students' attention and turning it toward the lesson's aim by raising a significant question

Even if the children in your class are quiet and cooperative, you still need to catch their attention. Thoughts are scattered in as many directions as there are students. Their minds are not blanks on which to write a lesson. Aimless thoughts need to be gathered in and focused toward the goal of the lesson.

Initial attention-getting may take only a few seconds. It may even occur before the class begins. An interesting fact to arouse curiosity, something to look at or listen to, something to do with paper and pencil. Even motion attracts, so the very act of holding up a visual or writing on the board is an attention-getter.

One teacher caught attention with a pan of sand topped by construction paper pyramids. Buried in the sand were time capsules of rolled paper tied with thread on which were items of historical background important to the lesson's Bible story. Students excavated these capsules and shared their findings.

A Junior Department in Louisville, Kentucky stimulated want-to with a large scale model of the tabernacle and incense burning in the room.

To show children that if God didn't write His Word down, it would be so mixed up we wouldn't have the true Word today, a West Bridgewater, Massachusetts teacher played "telephone." She whispered a sentence in a child's ear and each passed it on.

Another teacher used tape-recorded opinions of various people to arouse attention.

Attention, however, must become *intention.* The opening moments of the lesson must lead to something that takes on significance for students and becomes their goal. This means helping students feel a curiosity to have a question answered, a need to come to grips with an issue that has bearing on their everyday living, a need for the lesson at hand so that they will hang in there.

Who wouldn't like to teach a lesson on Sunday morning that is a direct answer to a student's question? It happens, but not often. Though we can't wait for children to ask the right questions, we can learn what our Middlers and Juniors are interested in and what their needs are.

A word of caution here: interests are not always needs. Boys may be interested in baseball, for example, but starting class with an animated discussion on baseball will seldom lead to consideration of a basic spiritual need. Do that outside class for rapport.

We need to know what our students are deeply concerned about, what they feel is important, what they want answers to. Then we can set up some way to focus their attention on this basic hunger-need and whet their appetites for what God has to fill that need. Children will not learn if they do not sense a need to learn.

What is suggested for *Focus* in your Teacher Manual for a given lesson may be just right. But if it isn't, exercise your skills and change the approach so that your students will become personally involved in the discovery process that follows.

DISCOVER: helping students discover God's answer by becoming involved with their Bibles

You have captured your students' attention and turned it toward the lesson's aim. You have raised a significant question that your students can make "their own." You have aroused the want-to. Now you come to the next part of the learning process: guiding your students in discovering God's answer to the question you have just raised.

You do this first by involving your students in a Bible narrative. Through an action-packed story students step vicariously into the sandals of a Bible character. They see a situation through his eyes; they feel, hear, touch, and sometimes even smell what he did.

In this part of the lesson you stretch students to listen with the intent to find an answer, to read the Bible for themselves, to make personal discoveries of what God has actually revealed of Himself and His ways of working.

Dealing with the story leads naturally to thinking through important concepts of God and His ways. After hearing or reading the whole story, students are ready to deal with the parts. Here you use thought-provoking questions, role playing, a teaching aid that involves thought, an assignment that leads students to compare Scripture with Scripture—something that enables students to make their own discoveries.

But this is not all. You want to guide your students in discovering what the Bible truth means to them personally. You will help them think through the possible implications for their own lives.

It is possible for students to become involved in the focus part of the lesson, but to lose that focus because the rest of the lesson is too diffused. Children need to feel that the lesson makes sense, that it is leading them to the goal, that they are learning. It helps to make verbal bridges to show how each activity relates to the goal. It helps to take time to summarize just a bit along the way. It helps to ask progress questions or use other means to check up so that learners feel successful.

It helps to make learners feel accepted by commending instead of correcting: "You are close to the answer, Jim. Keep thinking." It helps to relate what they are learning to life so that need-hunger is filled: "Think of something you want very much. What are wrong ways to get it? What are right ways? Why should you choose right ways when wrong ones are easier and faster?"

To keep the focus sharp throughout the lesson, use the Student Manual. It has the Bible story, the Bible look-ups, thought questions, situations pictured that help students discover the implications of the Bible truth. Use the teaching aid that goes with the lesson. Often it is just the tool you need to keep the lesson on track. The memory verse study is designed to help you summarize what your students are discovering. By memorizing the verse students are making the Bible truth their own.

Use all these learning devices because they help you move quickly and smoothly on to your destination: the response of your students to the Lord who has spoken to them through His Word.

RESPOND: helping students apply Bible truths to their lives and make obedient response to the Lord

Someone has said that the reason for our teaching God's Word in Sunday School is so that our students will become "Christ-governed persons." We capture interest, we focus attention on a significant question, we guide students into God's Word—it's a thrilling process, but it is only a process. The goal for our teaching is for our students to make a response to a Person—to the Lord Himself.

At the climax of class we wrap things up. The significant question which students made "their own," the Bible truth discovered, the implications discussed, all contribute toward helping students realize their need to respond in obedience to what they have learned.

You give your students opportunity to personalize the memory verse, to see themselves in a real-life situation described in the Student Manual, to manipulate a teaching aid, to write out a brief promise or prayer: all this is done to encourage students to make their response personal.

Then to nurture that response you need some carry-over into the week. The take-home paper has suggestions for daily Bible readings and an at-home activity that helps students recall the Bible truth and apply it throughout the week.

Focus, Discover, Respond—all parts of the *Guided Discovery Learning* approach to teaching. Three keys to the hearts of your students. These keys are discussed in more detail in the next chapters of this book.

Thinking it through

1. How would you explain to a new teacher the *Guided Discovery Learning* approach to instruction?

2. What ingredients help make an effective *Focus* part of a lesson?

3. Why is it important for learners to be actively involved in the *Discovery* part of a lesson?

4. In the *Respond* part of the lesson, what is the teacher's part? the learner's part, the Lord's part?

4
Teaching
Bible Facts
and Bible Truths

Teachers in one Junior Department exulted in studies of Paul's travels. Juniors made exciting maps. They named places Paul preached. They traced where he went and drilled on what he did. When they finished, each Junior could give an adequate account of Paul's missionary journeys—better than most adults.

Now compare this. In another Sunday School a 4th-grade class started with the problem of trouble. The class examined one of Paul's troubles. Since Paul was obeying the Lord, they asked, why did he have trouble? They asked more questions about trouble. They looked up some things God's Word has to say about trouble. They tried to understand why God allows trouble. Finally the class came to the question, "If we are obeying the Lord, but trouble comes our way, what should we do?" The stock answer is "Pray." But nine-year-old Cindy groped to express something different, "I'll remember—ah— God's thoughts and—ah—His ways are better than—ah mine." It is doubtful, however, that anyone in this class could trace Paul's journeys with passing accuracy.

Which class was more productive? Many may say the first learned more. Both were teaching God's Word. In teaching the Bible, what are we really after?

Facts are basic
Class number one was going after Bible facts. Think of assuring words to describe facts: accurate, proved, accepted, objective (apart

from my own mind), specific or precise, concrete (belonging to actual things and events). A fact is something solid you can grab because it is real.

Facts are the building blocks of knowledge. *Bible* facts are basic to *Bible* understanding. They give us the range of information which we need to get at what God is revealing in His Word.

And how Juniors do gobble up facts. One father felt the *Guinness Book of World Records* is the stuff Juniors are made of: What is the oldest known age for an elephant? Who ate the most hot dogs at one time? What is the world record for sneezing? Juniors like to be in the know. It gives them a feeling of power among their peers: "I know something you don't know." For Christian Juniors Bible quiz books are treasure tomes of facts: Who is the oldest man in the Bible? Who ate poison pottage and didn't die? Who stretched himself upon a dead boy until he sneezed seven times? Fact-gathering and its skills are a necessary prelude to thinking.

Of course, a collection of unrelated facts is not what Sunday School teachers major in. But Juniors must know what the Bible says, and it's a great age to give them the facts.

Get the facts

Let's go on a fact-finding hunt. Turn to Luke 4:14-30 in your Bible. Once Jesus was a guest teacher of a large class. And the class ended in a riot! Pick out five facts which you find in this account. There are many more.

You won't all list the same, but did you get a few of these: *Who?* Jesus; *Where?* Nazareth; *When:* synagogue worship; *What happened?* Jesus taught Isaiah 61:1-2; people pleased; no miracles; Gentile reference; Jews angry; murder attempt; Jesus escaped.

End of Scripture. End of Sunday School lesson? We hope not. When children know these facts, what do they know? When they have learned that Jesus taught He was the Messiah, but did no miracles and people tried to kill Him, they have learned the facts of what God *says*. But have they learned what God *means* in revealing the facts? Teaching the Bible is more than teaching a million facts! Someone has raised this searching question: If our pupils were to forget the *facts* of our lessons, what would they have left?

More than facts!

When you work a jigsaw puzzle, you interlock each piece with another. Now squeeze in the last piece. Eureka! The picture is complete. Just so the smaller what-happened Bible fact puzzle pieces fit together to form a larger, significant, transcendent, spiritual revelation. It doesn't need objective proof by scientists or historians because it doesn't belong to actual things and events. It is a subjective teaching or principle which is accepted personally by choice as true. We'll call it *Bible truth.*

Some question whether Juniors care one whit about going beyond Bible facts into Bible truths and whether they can do so.

Consider a list of questions one Junior girl presented a teacher in Milwaukee, Wisconsin. The girl had not yet accepted Christ as her personal Saviour but was seeking: *What is a soul? Why are we here? Why does God make bad people? Why did God make poor people? Why did God make rich people? Why did God make things to hurt people? Why does God make us lie? Why do you always think? Why did Jesus come? Why did God pick Jesus for His Son?* Was she concerned with Bible facts or Bible truths?

It is true some Middlers and Juniors are more reflective than others and more ready to dig into meaning. Some reach the ability to do relational thinking and reflective thinking ahead of others. You can see this unevenness in a class of nine-year-olds. Pat asks why Jesus wants us to give Him glory—what does "glory" mean? Another student brightens up. A third "sharpie" doesn't lift her head. The others look blank. Pat's question is beyond them. There's a bit of discussion and Pat says, "Oh, I see it now—ah, I guess I do!" No amount of probing will take Pat or the others any further because they are already stretching the limits of their development.

Identifying a Bible truth

Work a bit with the Bible puzzle facts in Luke 4:14-30 to see what Bible truth picture emerges. You'll see parts of the picture before you see the whole.

Is the "Bible truth" what Jesus taught? Partly. He undoubtedly explained Isaiah 61:1-2 as the Saviour-Messiah coming to the sin-sick, rather than the popular picture of the King-Messiah coming in power to make Israel world conquerors. The people found His words and manner pleasing. We have part of the picture.

Was it that Jesus said He was the Messiah? Partly. The learners were not upset at this point. They waited for proof. Show them and they would believe. That's another part of the picture.

But Jesus turned things around—believe and I will show you! He refused proof and by so doing showed up their lack of faith. Jesus never did miracles without faith. Another part of the picture. Put the parts together. You have it—faith is the whole picture.

That Jesus did no miracles in Nazareth is a fact. That *the Lord works on our behalf only in response to faith* is a Bible truth which the Holy Spirit reveals from the facts of the Scripture. We must get beyond the what-happened action to the why-it-happened picture of faith. What does it mean to have faith? Why do we need to believe and trust the Lord? How do we show we do?

Granted, we can't teach everything about faith in one lesson, but we can teach something. Hopefully this Bible truth on faith will be grouped with other Bible truths on faith to develop a concept of faith.

Ways to teach Bible facts

Bible facts are the input of data into our brain memory bank from all our senses. Such data comes from Bible stories and role playing and dialogues; from films, filmstrips, records, tape recordings, projected still material, picture studies, maps, charts, models, puppets, learning trips to places of interest; from interviews, and projects and research. . . . Are you breathless?

To help pupils remember more and forget less—or more accurately, to file facts in their memory banks for ready recall—takes effort, but the effort is a must for learning. Recent research shows the brain records only 13% of what we *hear*, but 76% of what we *see*. That really puts us in a spin!

Choose facts with care.   Sort Bible facts and rank-order them according to importance. Use only those Bible facts which make a significant contribution. Avoid overstuffing. One teacher uses a large spiral-bound sketch book for a flip chart. She prints the key question for the lesson and then outlines important facts from the Bible story to remember. Since she is inclined toward "overstuffing," it helps her

cut material as well as provide an easy story guide and review.
Box facts in meaning. We forget ideas that don't seem
important to us, facts not clear to us, and truths we don't make use of.
So give facts meaning by explaining them and relating them and
using them.

Teachers in Brockton, Massachusetts used an overhead projector
to talk about the Ten Commandments and had the pupils paraphrase
each commandment in a brief statement. During the discussion of
each commandment, the pupils gave illustrations from their own lives
or things they had heard. What God said took on meaning.

Wrap facts with excitement. We easily recall what is unexpected and fresh, what comes through exciting sensory input, what
stirs us to emotion, what gives us satisfaction and fulfillment. That's
why stories and visual media and discovery methods are so valuable.
They carry the impact of the new, the senses, the emotions, and the
climactic. The facts become desirable, eagerly accepted "gifts."

Kathy, a Junior in Elgin, Illinois, with some talent for music and
poetry, wrote "God Made Them," a song about Creation. Juniors
learned the song and illustrated it on a wall mural. Her teacher made
a recording of them singing the song and took a picture of the Juniors
under the mural. That's really wrapping facts in excitement!

Use facts often. A valuable, exciting gift is a pleasure to recall. The
oftener the recall, the easier the recall. A teacher from Barrington,
Rhode Island used some of these methods to review Bible information and memory work:

Matching   Print a question or the first part of a verse on one
card, and the answer or last part of the verse and reference on
another card. Distribute one or more cards to each pupil. The one
with the question or the beginning part of the verse reads it; the one
with the second part of the verse or answer responds.

Puzzle Wheel Review   Cut two circles of cardboard, one
four or five inches larger than the other. Fasten the circles together
at the center with a brass fastener (small circle on top) so that both
circles turn. Divide the circles into eighths by drawing lines
through the center to the edge. Print half of a verse, or a question
on the outside or bottom circle. Print the other half of the verse or
answer to the question on the inside top circle. Each child takes

turns choosing a verse or question and revolving the sections to complete the verse or question.

Fish Bowl Review   Print memory verse references or questions on cardboard fish. Attach paper clips to noses of the fish and place them in a fishbowl. Let each pupil "fish" with a small magnet attached to a string from the end of a stick. The first fish hooked must be drawn up. If correctly answered, the pupil keeps that fish.

Another idea is to print the questions or references on tissue paper fish and let pupils draw up the fish by sucking in on a straw.

Ways to teach Bible truths

It is one thing for one's brain memory bank to master specific factual data which is easily labeled and filed and recalled. It is quite another thing to grab onto something like "faith" which floats out there in space almost like an ethereal bubble, ready to go puff. The key to gaining insight into Bible truths is to give them substance. Find out what they are made up of. Take them apart and put meaning into how they are formed. Bring them down to earth.

A solid foundation   It's as simple as ABC that you start with what students know, then guide them in discovering what they don't know. Building on the known gives the unknown Bible truth solid foundation.

Suppose your Bible truth is "Trust in God, not money." Children know about money, but have hardly considered whether they put their trust in it or not. Try this foundation: "Here's a quarter. It says, 'In God we trust.' If you want something at the store, you have to hand over the quarter. Why shouldn't the quarter say, 'In money we trust'? Why should we trust God rather than the quarter when it is the quarter which gets us what we want, whether it's our parents' money or money we earn?"

Bible truth in Bible action   Bring Bible truth down to earth by showing it in concrete action. The story of the rich young man of Mark 10:17-22 shows how Jesus let this young man know which he was trusting, the Lord or money. This experience acted out in front of Jesus' class showed them the Bible truth about which to trust. Tell the story and your class will be back there with Jesus' class, learning in the same way His did.

Visualize Bible truth. After His class experienced the action, Jesus used an analogy: It is easier for a camel to go through the eye of a needle than for a rich man to enter into the kingdom of God. Everybody understood that. Perhaps there was a camel on the scene. You might use Jesus' object lesson with a picture of a camel or horse and a needle. It might be more effective for Middlers to stack up pennies as bars of gold or use a coin bank to separate a stand-up figure of a boy or girl from a Bible to represent God.

Explore meaning. Jesus and His class also had a discussion about putting trust in money. Encourage more mature Juniors to share ideas, look up what God says, give examples. Talk *with* Juniors, not *at* them. If the young man couldn't be saved by giving away riches, why did Jesus ask him to give all his away? Doesn't God want us to have nice things? If we need something, how do we get it?

Relate Bible truth to experience. Program your computer brain to read out some personal experiences of how God took care of your needs. This gets Middler and Junior computers clicking to recall theirs.

Do something. The clincher is to try out the Bible truth in life to experience it firsthand. Students may think of something they want, decide if it is "need or greed," and then how they will get it. Or they may complete true-to-life case studies to think how God could supply needs.

Notice how each of these suggestions does basically the same thing. It brings the "floating" Bible truth down to earth and gives it concrete substance by putting meaning into it.

And then there are concepts

Suppose you were knee high to a grasshopper and spent Sunday after Sunday under a watchful giant-size eye painted in living color inside a triangle on the ceiling of your church. And suppose you had just memorized the Scripture, "Thou God seest me." What would be your idea of God? Would you find that "eye" disconcerting, as if a cough or dropped hymnbook would make it glare? A child whose idea of God is *only* a watchful eye to spy on him responds differently to God than a child whose idea of God is a caring, helping Shepherd. Two different concepts.

A concept is simply the idea we have of anything and everything, tangible and intangible—the way we conceive of it or think of it. Without a concept of love and forgivensss, how can we know a God of love and forgiveness?

Bible truths and Bible concepts are two sides of the same coin. Bible truth is what the teacher is teaching and Bible concept is the idea the pupil is receiving from the teaching.

They're all mine. Concepts are highly individualistic. They are made up of many impressions, feelings, ideas, thoughts which form through our world of senses. Everyone's life is unique and so are his concepts.

Nobody can see them. A teacher can't get at a pupil's total concept of any Bible truth no matter how much he digs. Concepts are known only by their effects in words and deeds. Even those are misleading. Don't assume a student has a concept simply because he talks or acts as if he does. He may be imitating. A student may talk about "sin," but have only a vague idea of what it is and no idea that it includes him. On the other hand, we must not assume children don't understand what they can't explain or put into use. You don't have to explain forgiveness to ask forgiveness.

They're building all the time. Concept-building is going on constantly. Our brains are so structured by the Lord that they keep revising and reorganizing ideas as new data is fed in.

What's a teacher to do? Let's take an example. You are ready to teach the Bible truth "all have sinned." First check on your Juniors' concept (idea) of sin. Ask them, "What is sin?" Most will reveal their impressions in the answer: "Killing, stealing, lying, swearing." Notice two things: They have answered with specific acts of sin and they have named more than one act. This is because they still think literally, but have arrived at a very important mental ability, that of being able to group or classify.

Is their concept of sin adequate? No, it's functional, but too limited. It probably excludes their particular sins if they are reasonably "good." Because of their limited idea, they may have no real concept of sin as applying to everyone.

You may expand their idea of sin by listing more sins: disobeying, cheating, fighting, hating—all likely to occur in the life of every

Junior. You may also draw a horizontal line to represent God's perfect standard. They know what it means to be perfect. Then below it draw vertical lines of varying heights with none reaching the horizontal line. Children know what it means to "measure up." No one measures up to God's perfection (Rom. 3:23).

Now do your students have an adequate concept of the Bible truth "all have sinned"? Ask them who "all" means. "Everyone." "Does that include you, and you, and you—and me?" They may hesitate to say that the teacher is a sinner, but if they say it, they probably understand the concept "all have sinned."

And then there are values

Values are deeply held personal beliefs and convictions. They mold what we are and motivate what we do. They are our goal-setters and designers of life.

The what and how of values The "what" of values is the *content* of our beliefs and convictions. It would seem to follow that to teach the content of values we should transmit the content of God's Word. But there is more to values. There is also the "how" of values or the *process* by which we form our beliefs and convictions. Values are formed by interaction between "value-makers" and "value-accepters."

Value-makers Who are the ones responsible for values? The Lord says it is the parents, particularly fathers (Deut. 6:1-9), and research bears this out. Rather than just handing value-content to children, the Lord instructs parents to follow a value-process of living out values. They are to model values by example, visualize them, speak of them, discuss them.

But parents are not the sole value-makers in today's society. Middlers and Juniors spend much time interacting with age-mates. Their peer group develops its own set of values and applies its own pressures.

And let's not forget ubiquitous television. Its commercials, its heroes with flesh and blood reality, its lifestyles—all subtly model values and woo identification with them.

Value-accepters According to Dr. Lawrence Kohlberg's studies, children go through three predictable sequences in developing moral values. In Level I a child accepts "good" as anything which helps him and "bad" as anything which hurts him. He is guided by reward and punishment.

In Level II a youngster is able to separate good and bad from self-gratification. He accepts as right whatever pleases significant persons in his life. He is guided by rules for right and wrong.

In Level III a young person is able to think of right and wrong in terms of moral principles and can generalize these principles.

Not everyone arrives at Level III. Some develop no further than Level II, accepting others' wishes and rules as their guide to values. Some even remain at Level I, with self-gratification as their only guide to values.

So where do teachers fit? A class at Sunday School cannot provide the real-life experiences of a home. It prepares for life rather than lives life. And yet a teacher can *help* develop values in a class situation.

1. Know families. Since families are the strong value-makers, know what values are being built into your students. Visit homes, have parent-teacher meetings, listen as students express parental views.

2. Model values. Teachers continually send value messages. Some may be negative. Sarcasm or broken promises say, "You don't really matter to me." Lack of preparation translates to "God's Word is not valuable to me." An untidy classroom suggests, "Teaching is not worth my time."

Value messages should be positive. A teacher who gives generously of self models the value of unselfishness. A teacher who exhibits trust models the value of Christian faith.

3. Study God's value-content. These are excellent years for understanding God's laws and moral precepts. Juniors have usually reached that stage of mental and moral development where they see the need for rules. They can look beyond pleasing self to pleasing others. They have a strong sense of justice. One authority says that if moral precepts are not built now, they may never be. But we need to take heed—to know a rule does not guarantee that it will be internalized as a value in personality. But it is a step.

4. Ask, "What do you think?" Instead of a closed "Do as I say" atmosphere, teach in an open "What do you think?" atmosphere. Dr. Kohlberg offers four factors that contribute to development of moral judgment:

(a) Experiences of justice—right and wrong with consequences

(b) Experiences of social interaction—hearing other points of view

(c) Open discussion of moral concerns—saying what they think

(d) Opportunities for role playing—trying out with words and actions what they think

Though teachers cannot offer firsthand experiences in doing right and wrong, they can guide students in working out rules. They can pose true-to-life problems, stimulate inquiry, examine issues in the light of God's Word, exchange views, ask why, think through various lines of action and their consequences.

5. *Role play.* In role play students put themselves in the shoes of imagined persons. By acting out the values of these persons, they recognize the consequences of right and wrong actions.

6. *Give approval.* When a student expresses a biblical value in word or action, help him hold onto it by giving approval. In this way we help make the action important, satisfying, memorable, and worth trying again.

7. *Rely on the Holy Spirit.* The Holy Spirit is the ultimate Value-Maker. He works through the value-content of the Word and the value-process of the Lord, that process which is characterized by interaction of the value-maker and the value-accepter.

Thinking it through

1. Try to explain to another person the difference between teaching Bible facts and teaching Bible truths.

2. Look at a lesson in your curriculum. Pick out and state the Bible truth.

3. Which of the ways to teach Bible truths (pp. 28-29) have you already used? Which will you try out?

4. Try to describe your childhood idea of God in a few sentences.

5. Look at the list of questions asked by the Junior girl under "More than facts" (p. 25). Which indicate inadequate concepts that need careful teaching of Bible truth?

6. What is your reaction to this statement, "Values are transmitted

by word of mouth"? If it is inadequate, how are values developed? Who are value-makers in our society?

7. At which of Dr. Kohlberg's levels of moral development do your students appear to be? Why is the Junior age such an important time for developing values?

8. Use the ways teachers help develop values (pp. 32-33) to rate yourself. Are you strong on developing values? Weak? In between?

5
Motivating through Stories

Excitement ran high as Juniors arrived at Sunday School. A missionary conference was beginning. But with extra announcements, the children were beginning to fidget when the special speaker was finally introduced. Looking at his guest, the superintendent felt dubious. Somehow the missionary seemed too fragile for her task of commanding the attention of 60 restless Juniors. His heart sank as she began to speak—barely above a whisper! But the Juniors sat transfixed. Later, nine-year-old David confided, "The whole time she was up there I didn't blink my eyes once!"

What had focused the attention of the youngsters? Colorful visuals? Puppets? Magic? No, she had simply told a story.

What's in a story?
A story can transport listeners across boundaries of time and space, can get a child out of his self-centered world and provide him with an unforgettable vicarious experience. A story can communicate a profound insight, illustrate a weighty truth, deepen a child's understanding of himself, motivate change of behavior, develop attitudes, and arouse response to our great God. A story can do many things, and the Master Storyteller is Jesus.

Walk with Him along dusty roads of Palestine. Sit with Him in a gently rocking fishing boat. Rest with Him on a hillside—and listen. Jesus used stories to:

- captivate the masses (Luke 8:4)
- confront people with their needs (10:25-37; 12:13-21)
- teach about His Father (11:1-13)
- answer His accusers (15:1-32)
- communicate principles of right living (16:1-13)
- correct misunderstandings (19:11-27)
- answer questions (20:1-19).

Why Bible stories?

It's Promotion Sunday. Eight new students come into your class bursting with enthusiasm and curiosity. Getting to know you, their teacher, is high on their priority list. They'll probably ask questions that startle you with their undisguised frankness. In addition, they'll observe you closely. It's almost uncanny how they'll see beyond what you say about yourself to what you show of yourself in your actions and responses. More than one teacher has commented with chagrin, "You can't put anything over on those kids. They see you for what you are!" On the other hand, more than one Middler and Junior has chosen to follow Jesus, persuaded by his teacher's life more than by what his teacher said.

God in infinite wisdom has chosen to reveal Himself through the written Word. He has given many direct statements about Himself, of course, but much of Scripture is in narrative form. There are stories of birth and death, love and hate, peace and war—exciting stories, comforting stories, colorful insights into the humanness of us all. But there's more—vastly more. For those stories tell not only about characters and events but also reveal God and His ways. Through those stories we come to know God *as we see Him in action*.

God has placed in your hands a tremendous teaching tool in revealing Himself through stories. The sublime epistle truths are often too abstract for literal-thinking Middlers and Juniors. Much of the imagery and beauty in the poetic and prophetic Books goes over their heads, but stories children can grasp. And these stories are God's authoritative Word. You can use Bible stories to:

- show through actual events God's ability to meet needs
- gain insights into God and His ways of working
- trace how God worked out His plan of redemption

- discover how God revealed Himself to someone in Bible times
- contrast the tragic consequences of disobeying God with the joyous outcomes of obeying Him
- observe God at work fulfilling His purposes behind the rise and fall of nations.

So many stories—how do I choose?

How do you go about choosing a Bible story? The simple answer: with your listeners in mind. Jesus never told a story just to be telling it. He knew His listeners' thoughts and needs, and He reached them with just the right stories.

Lacking Jesus' supernatural discernment, you'll probably follow the suggestions of your curriculum publisher, relying on the Holy Spirit to take His Word and speak to your pupils. You can know generally, of course, what stories will appeal by keeping in mind characteristics of your listeners.

They want action.   So you'll look for stories that involve people going places and doing things.

They go for adventure.   The Bible has a bountiful supply of stories filled with suspense. And because your students' world is widening rapidly, they are ready to hear the major Bible narratives in their years in the Middler and Junior Departments.

They are ready to get the big picture.   You'll paint in the finer deails of Bible background to give pupils the sense of where the event took place, what the times were like, and how the story fits chronologically with other events studied.

They want a story that goes somewhere.   You'll keep a definite Bible truth in mind, avoiding parenthetical details that would sidetrack your listeners.

They can probe behind the scenes.   You'll show what God was about in the lives of people.

How do I get ready to tell the story?

When to start?   A teacher shares her formula for preparing to tell the Bible story, "Slow down; start early." She explains, "First, I read the story slowly several times. I get acquainted with the characters, see their actions, hear what they are saying, feel their emotions, and search out the truth God is revealing through that story. No Saturday night preparation for me. I start early in the week."

She avoids cramming to get details fixed in her mind. By Sunday she has the story so well thought through that she is free to adapt it to the time available in class. And she's free to watch the faces of her pupils to spot a question in a child's eyes and quickly weave in just the right clarifying word or phrase.

Perhaps it helps to think of a storyteller as a painter. Instead of paints and brushes he's working with words and his voice. With these he paints a three-dimensional picture, a moving picture at that!

The words you use   As you get ready to tell the story you'll choose action verbs that provide movement. And the more specific your verbs the more precisely your students will see the picture. For example, a traveler could go, hike, run, stalk, ramble, march, plod, or shuffle. Each verb changes the visual image your listeners have of the traveler.

You'll search out sensory words that give texture, color, taste, feeling. And you'll use direct dialogue whenever possible to develop your characters.

And then there's your voice   Practice your story aloud to discover the various effects you can get. Try recording your story. You'll enjoy learning to change tones for different characters. Notice how a pause can indicate passage of time, anticipate the beginning of a new scene, or build suspense.

Keeping your story moving.   You'll want to avoid interrupting your story, even with rhetorical questions. A teacher was doing very well with his story until he came to the climax. Hoping to build suspense, he paused and asked, "And what do you think happened next?" His class welcomed this as a literal request to anticipate the next scene. They contributed with imaginative flare, and the few who listened when the teacher finally picked up his story again felt let down. The real story wasn't nearly so much fun!

What about visuals?   They're the greatest when they do what the spoken word can't do. You'll be on the lookout constantly for pictures, diagrams, maps, and models. You want every possible aid to clarify customs, pinpoint where events occurred, and bring the Bible account to life. Whether you show the visual as you tell the story or use it separately depends on the visual and the impact it will have on the class. If the visual takes your students on a detour from the story line, it would be used better in another part of the lesson.

Should I memorize the story?   Skilled storytellers share their secret: "Live" the story so that you can tell it without actually memorizing it. However, there may be exact Scripture quotations and short passages that need to be given word perfect. These you will want to memorize. Many teachers also find it helpful to learn by heart those important opening words that capture attention and the closing words that bring the story to a satisfying end.

"I know that already!"   A blunt complaint from one in the class is disconcerting when you've carefully prepared to tell your Bible story. It's true, after attending Sunday School and Vacation Bible School for six to nine years, Middlers and Juniors will know a good many of the Bible narratives. Should you insist that they listen to the story told in the same familiar way one more time?

You can look, instead, at the Scripture, asking the Lord for fresh insight, a new point of view, a way of involving students in discovering meaning.

Turning the Bible account of Solomon's spiritual decline into personal diary entries, for example, helps children feel the emptiness and waste of his life. Letting pupils become citizens of Jerusalem questioning Peter in the days following Pentecost will help them capture the wonder of the Holy Spirit's work in transforming fearful disciples into bold witnesses.

A teacher in Massachusetts brought Noah's experience right into the world of her pupils. She skillfully put the ark right in the center of their city, "on the green," and had them imagine their pastor building it. Her children "heard" the ridicule and "saw" the scoffers. Then they understood better what it means to obey God by faith.

Then what about me, *the storyteller?*   The best answer is to forget yourself! Which would you rather have students say, "My teacher is a great storyteller," or "That was a great story"? Obviously you'll choose the latter. A painter doesn't concern himself with what people think of the way he holds his brush or how he splashes color on his canvas. He's concentrating on his picture. Similarly, you'll want to wrap yourself as completely as possible in the plot, hide yourself in the characters, and immerse yourself in the action, prayerfully expecting God to speak to hearts as you do your part.

And when it's over   Though you stop telling the story at just the right point—never with a sermon added—you'll see to it that the story does not stop. Through creative methods, such as those described in the next chapter, you'll get your Middlers and Juniors deeper into the action, probing the message and meaning of the story, discovering God, and thinking through what their response to Him should be.

Thinking it through

1. How did Jesus use stories to good advantage?

2. How do stories in the Bible help us come to know God?

3. Stories can do more than provide entertainment. Tell several ways you can use stories to teach truth. Check these ways with the ones listed on pages 36 and 38.

4. Getting ready to tell a story is an important part of lesson preparation. Write a checklist you can use in getting ready to tell a story.

6
Guiding
Students in Discovery

"I like that teacher. He makes us think!"

"If God really is love, why is there so much killing in the Bible? It is just like today."

"Our fourth-graders don't read their Sunday School papers in church anymore during the pastor's message. They have to find out if the pastor is telling the truth or not."

What's going on here? These boys and girls are turned on to "discovering" Bible truth!

dis.cov.er 2: to obtain sight or knowledge of for the first time: FIND.

. . . syn ASCERTAIN, DETERMINE, UNEARTH, LEARN: DISCOVER presupposes exploration, investigation, or chance encounter and always implies the previous existence of what becomes known; . . . LEARN may imply acquiring knowledge with little effort or conscious intention (as by simply being told); it may imply study and practice, but usually does not stress active search. *(Webster's Seventh New Collegiate Dictionary)*

Did you ever consider what a before-His-time educator Jesus was? Two thousand years ago He was doing what educators are promoting today as if they had invented it. And, though it did not seem so at that time, Jesus was the most successful Educator of all time. His students set the world on fire!

Read the definition carefully. Which was Jesus concerned with— "active search" or "passive acceptance"?

Operation upset

Jewish education was as stereotyped as . . . well, as some of our teaching! The role of a student was to accept without question, memorize, conform. The result was spiritual ignorance and sterile practice. Jesus struggled mightily against legalistic leaders who insisted on blind and passive acceptance of their interpretations of God's Word. He had some choice names for the Pharisees: "vipers," "hypocrites," "whited sepulchers full of dead men's bones."

Jesus was busy probing, uncovering, stirring, enlightening, challenging to reaction and action in a turnabout way. This was simply not done in His day! Jesus' point was to get student participation and involvement so that the feedback opened up learners to reveal weakness, shallowness, error. When they gained personal insight they were ready for relationship with God through faith in Jesus. Closed, passive pupils may appear to take in truth, but they don't change as a result of the truth. Open, actively searching pupils do. Jesus was out to change people from inside out.

Think!

One of the most fascinating aspects of Jesus' teaching was the way He demanded that learners wrestle with truth.

The parables were puzzling: "The kingdom of heaven is like a mustard seed" (Matt. 13:31, NIV).

Analogies were often difficult: "I am the Bread of life" (John 6:35).

Stories turned into problems: "Which of these three do you think was a neighbor to the man who fell into the hands of robbers?" (Luke 10:36, NIV)

Ordinary statements were challenged: "Good teacher . . ." said one. Jesus countered, "Why do you call Me good? . . . No one is good— except God alone" (18:18-19, NIV).

Sabbath laws fell to the hammer of His logic: "You hypocrites! Doesn't each of you on the Sabbath untie his ox or donkey from the stall and lead it out to give it water?" (13:15, NIV)

The next time you read the Gospels try underlining everything

Jesus did or said which made learners think.

Now, how will you get students to think? They are beginning thinkers. Some don't even know yet that they like to wrestle with thoughts. Most are not used to digging below the surface. They think concretely and literally, rather than abstractly. But they think and can love it! Learning to see relationships and come to conclusions strengthens faith. It does not destroy it.

What's in a question?   Draw a line from each question to what it does for a student.

What do you think people outside the ark did when the Flood came?	• provokes thought
	• stirs imagination and curiosity
How long had Noah been in the ark?	
	• calls for conclusion
Why didn't people pay attention to God's warning and repent?	• gets attention
	• recalls fact
In our day of increased crime, will God again destroy everything in a flood? Why, or why not?	
What will happen when people get this rotten again?	

What's the answer to this question: Is the main truth we learn from the Flood story that God keeps His promises? That's a leading question with a yes-no answer. Better avoid it.

How about this question: Which did Noah send out first—the dove or the raven? You're calling for a choice which encourages guessing. Don't waste your time.

And this question: How did Noah know when to go into the ark and when did it start raining? That's a double question. Take them one at a time. Here are a few success tips from teachers:

- Ask the question before calling on someone to answer. That way everyone has to think.
- Spread questions around to all students, but ask less mature children factual questions and more mature students the thought questions.
- Don't repeat questions or answers. If you do, everyone waits for the reruns.
- Try to get pupils to give thinking answers, not just a lazy word or two.

Open up a problem.   Phrase a problem in the form of a question and print it out for easy reference. Discuss possible solutions or answers. Get into the Bible story to see how God worked it out. Pinpoint God's answer. Think of ways to make God's solution work in life. Here's a possible development:

TEACHER: How do you feel when you do right?

JOAN: I feel good inside.

TEACHER: Does doing right always make you feel happy?

JACK: Not me!

TEACHER: Why do you say that, Jack?

JACK: The guys sometimes make fun of me!

ART: Yeah! I returned a dollar I found and everyone said I was dumb!

BETTY: If you're always good, kids think you're gross. You get teased a lot.

TEACHER: Then, if doing right can make you unhappy, why do right? Let's print that problem on the chalkboard. There was a young man in the Bible who did right and just got a lot of trouble in return. *(Class studies story of Joseph sold as slave.)*

Be reflective.   One class tape-recorded first-person reflections of people in their Bible story. Juniors went back to the Bible for clues. Then they had each Bible character talk about his thoughts and actions, speaking in the first person.

Get juniors buzzing.   Divide your class into two or three groups of Juniors. Give each a written question, problem, or Bible look-up activity. Move chairs into small huddle groups. Designate a capable leader for each group who will report results. Since most students work faster when faced with the challenge of time, after being sure each group knows its task, give a signal for "go." Keep an eye on the clock and call for "time" at the end of your announced limit. Or set a timer or alarm. Call for reports.

A question-and-answer chart   After introducing a new subject, encourage Middlers or Juniors to think of everything they would like to know about it. For example, if you are studying about witnessing, think of questions concerning what we should tell, how we can go about witnessing, why missionaries go to other countries, what to do if someone makes fun of us, what to do if we don't have answers. Print the questions on a large sheet of paper, leaving space for brief answers to be filled in as the unit progresses.

Teacher plays the opposition   A teacher in Westfield, Massachusetts points out that Juniors love to defend their point of view. She takes the opposite stand from what they know to be biblical truth and then challenges them to prove her wrong. She asks questions and reasons and presses for proof: What makes you so sure? Tell me what God says. What does that mean?

Encourage feedback

A teacher who gets plenty of feedback from fourth-graders says: "When a child enters my class I explain that we all think differently and God created us this way. We are not just a bunch of puppets God moves around. Repetition of this assurance that God does not expect us to think alike soon gives courage to each one to speak out just as he feels, knowing that no one will laugh. It is amazing how soon the children express themselves openly, even their doubts and fears, which they normally hide."

That atmosphere of acceptance and individual worth is basic to securing spontaneous response. It's also basic to spiritual growth. Boys and girls (and all of us) shrivel in a climate of disapproval. It threatens our well-being and shoves us back into the mold of sterile conformity.

The setting helps.   If the physical setting says the teacher is the "big jug" pouring truth into receptive "little mugs," there's not likely to be much feedback. Straight chairs in rows and the teacher behind a desk or podium says in so many words that learners are to drink in, not give forth. You'll induce response quicker with a face-to-face setting, circle, semicircle, or around a table, with the teacher as a member of the group. Attractive room, comfortable seating, correct temperature and lighting, unhurried pace are all part of relaxing tensions and creating openness.

Prime the pump. Middlers and Juniors will respond when the subject being discussed is close to their interests, problematic, real to them, and lends itself to varying responses. But sometimes it helps to prime the pump with personal experience, a visual which stimulates discussion, a news item, or a sharply divided yes-no issue.

Use questions that draw out. Try some of these: "How do you know?" "What would be an example?" "Is this what you're trying to say . . .?" "would you tell us more about that?"

Accept something from each answer. These comments say thanks for trying: "You've made an interesting point. Let's hear what others have to say." "That's part of the answer. Can you give us more?" "Good try, but the point you have made fits better with the next question. Let's hold onto it." "That's a new idea. We're glad for new ideas."

There's no put-down here. Every contribution is worth something, and when a pupil's thoughts are accepted as of worth, *he* feels accepted and ready to try again.

Make it productive. Anything you can do to show that what pupils are contributing leads to the goal promotes more feedback. Be alert to show that one point relates to another, that an idea has deeper implications. Keep your comments to a minimum—no lectures if you want feedback. Ask another child to comment or tell what he thinks. Summarize briefly as you go along so that students can see they are making progress.

Search!

Do you remember that after hearing the parable of the sower, Jesus' disciples came to Him asking the meaning of the parable? (Luke 8:4-15) Searching the Scriptures for themselves is most important for Juniors. But it is a new skill to be taught in easy steps and carefully nurtured. Teachers continually ask, "How do you get today's kids to use their Bibles to search the Scriptures at home?"

Middlers and Juniors need encouragement to make the Scriptures "their own" through personal search and discovery. Their take-home Bible assignments can do much to guide their search, but they need the friendly interest of a teacher to keep them motivated.

A teacher in Toronto, Ontario often closes her lesson with a teaser, such as, "I wish we had time to talk about another verse. It was such a help to me the other day when I needed it." The girls write down the reference and can hardly wait to read the verse and discover how it helped their teacher.

In Roslyn, Pennsylvania a teacher who takes her girls home to lunch on summer Sundays to do Bible study together, also mails reminders to do home Bible assignments.

Boys in a Glen Ellyn, Illinois church looked forward to "make-up day," a Saturday when they went to their teacher's home to make up any incomplete lessons and to discuss Bible-related questions.

What are these teachers doing? They are getting their students to use their Bibles outside the classroom. They are having them practice some of the Bible search skills they are learning in Sunday School.

A "Look and Listen" learning center can be a tremendous asset in your department. Try one which includes a record player, tape recorder, filmstrip projector which youngsters can operate; Bible handbooks and dictionaries with colorful maps, diagrams, and photographs; Bible storybooks, special magazines, and so on. Stock the corner with Bible background filmstrips and recordings, recorded stories, tape-recorded interviews with the pastor, for example, to answer a sticky question which came up in class the week before. Keep a bulletin board going with up-to-date news and pictures which relate to the unit being studied. Make use of the corner, not only before Sunday School begins, but during class by all or some students going to the table to find answers to questions.

Visualize

Visuals can be used at any point in a lesson, because they help illustrate truths when words fall short. They encourage children to "discover" Bible truth. Jesus used objects at hand to illustrate His teaching: birds and lilies, soil and stones and thorns, bread and water and sand and coins—and a host of others. Middlers and Juniors cannot only look at visuals to discover meaning, they can manipulate

visuals, create visuals, and use them to express Bible truth in their own words.

Manipulate visuals. Children come to life whenever there is action. They look with interest at a visual held up, but they immerse themselves in one which allows them a part of the action. Juniors and mature Middlers can sort word cards or pictures for preference or progression. They may build up a visual piece by piece to arrive at a whole. They may manipulate objects or arrange parts on a table, sort ideas or statements into boxes, tack pieces in correct order on a bulletin board, magnetic board, or flannelboard. The ways to manipulate teaching aids are almost endless.

Explain visuals. It is often difficult for Middlers and Juniors to grapple with abstract Bible truth. They need help putting ideas into their own words. Using a visual as a guide helps them understand what God means.

After a teacher in Idaho gave a flannelgraph presentation of the functions of each Person of the Trinity, Juniors tried to explain the Trinity in their own words. The teacher commented, "At first they were unsure of what to say and I had to draw out their response. Then a boy began putting up the figures, explaining as he did so, and he did very well."

A teacher in Indiana showed two of her girls how to present a simple object lesson using a fragile toothpick (me) made strong when coupled with a nail (the Holy Spirit). She commented, "Youngsters like to be involved. They get the point."

Create visuals. If you have ample time, what could be better than letting students discover Bible truth by capturing it in some visualized form they originate themselves? They may express what they are learning by creating posters, collages, rebuses, bulletin boards, murals, picture rolls, diagrams, displays, dioramas, banners, puppets, and many more.

The important point to remember is that the activity must always serve the goal of helping pupils discover and express Bible truth. Therefore they need to create with Bibles "at ready" for continual reference. They need teachers who know how to use creative activity to guide thinking and produce genuine learning. A teacher who lets students originate travel posters about heaven, for example, but converses about World Series baseball games while doing it is not using the activity for "discovery learning." But the teacher with a store of Bible references on heaven, questions, and illustrations, ready to use for discussion to guide creative expression, is making the activity serve as a means to the end—discovery.

Express ideas

Creative expression may be verbal as well as graphic, though some students may have negative feelings about writing and worry about the correctness of what they say. A wise teacher provides reassuring support that written ideas will not be judged for spelling and sentence structure or be graded. We are sharing thoughts to express what we understand about the Lord and what the Lord means to us personally.

Boys in a New England class wrote down what Jesus Christ meant to them while the pianist played quiet music to provide an atmosphere of thoughtful meditation. Each wrote approximately six sentences. What a delight to read genuine expressions of love for the Lord, assurance of salvation, and glimpses of personal needs. The testimonies guided this teacher in reaching deeper into the lives of these youngsters.

A teacher in Brockton, Massachusetts used a simulated TV newscast. Pupils studied the lesson ahead to prepare for teacher-led, taped interviews of Bible characters. After the newscast, teacher and pupils held a "critic's review," discussing which was fact and which was fiction to point out mistakes. This was followed by a commentary session when pupils could talk about the Bible account and relate their thoughts and feelings to those of the Bible characters.

Another teacher tells of the *Jerusalem Times* her class produced around Easter. They dated it "Good Friday" because the class felt they were less familiar with Jesus' suffering and dying for our sins than with events of His resurrection. Items included "Curtain Is Torn," "Earthquake Hits Jerusalem," "Barabbas Set Free" (exclusive interview), Passion Week events (research on traditional Jewish celebration). The newspaper also included a crossword puzzle, sports page of events from Roman sports, editorial page and death notices with a paragraph on each thief crucified, and Jesus. The class mimeographed the paper and gave copies to others in the Sunday School.

Experience

Experience is the stuff discovering is made of. There was Martha chewing out Mary for not being helpful. There was the storm with frightened disciples accusing Jesus of not caring enough to help them. Jesus turned these and other real life experiences into learning situations, ever ready to seize opportunity.

Jesus also used planned experience. He sent out the seventy on a tour to proclaim the Messiah. They returned with the joy of success, and Jesus enriched their experience by adding more teaching.

Jesus also used observation experience. He and His class observed the way people gave their offerings in the temple. Jesus used the widow and her mite as a living object lesson.

Use life-situation experiences. If you mingle with children before and after class and share with them on other occasions, you'll find yourself "teaching" informally and spontaneously as Jesus did so many times.

Plan experiences. Look over the Bible truths you are teaching. Can any of them be discovered by direct experience, such as sacrificial giving, witnessing, helping each other and those in need, praying together? With prayer and a little imagination you can plan projects beyond the Sunday School hour which will turn Bible truths into memorable learning.

Share personal experiences. When you share your dreams and disappointments, successes and failures, and how the Lord meets your needs, corrects and strengthens you, you are making Bible truth come alive through you so your pupils can experience it vicariously. You are not detracting from God's Word; you are illustrating how it is being used by the Holy Spirit in a dynamic way today.

In a recent poll Juniors reported that they like it best when their teacher tells stories about themselves. Juniors open up and tell things they would never tell anyone else when they know their teacher is sharing with them.

Contrive experience. Sometimes you can act out experiences to heighten reality. By putting yourself in the shoes of Bible people

and going through their experiences with them, you help the Bible become intensely alive and meaningful.
Transforming lives is an inside-out process, not an outside-in process. Jesus broke away from traditional telling and memorizing to stir up learners to be responsive, and the Holy Spirit blessed His methods. Why don't you give them a try?

Thinking it through

1. How did Jesus use *Guided Discovery Learning* in His ministry?
2. Give a few ideas for getting your students to think.
3. Why is feedback important in *Guided Discovery Learning?*
4. Visuals are usually used by teachers as aids to presenting a Bible lesson. How can students use visuals?
5. Look at some ways teachers helped their students express ideas, on page 51. Have you tried any of these? Can you add to them?
6. Thumb through the Gospels and make a list of real-life experiences which Jesus used for teaching.

7
Aiming for
Personal Response

"I don't like most Sunday Schools!" Cheryl was making no idle declaration. Her father's occupation required frequent moves, and Cheryl had probably attended a dozen different Sunday Schools.

Curious, her teacher invited her to explain.

With typical sixth-grade succinctness, Cheryl responded, "In most Sunday Schools they tell you what you already know and want you to do what you already know you should be doing. But in this class you make us use what we already know to find something new in the Bible. Then you make us let the Lord tell us what He wants us to do about it."

"Thank you, Cheryl, and thank You, Lord!" her teacher breathed inwardly.

Cheryl had grasped experientially what *Guided Discovery Learning* is all about. Though Cheryl wasn't aware of it, her teacher was prayerfully preparing Bible lessons to accomplish just this goal!

Each week the teacher focused attention on a pertinent life issue. She raised a significant question and channeled student energies to find God's answer as they listened to the Bible story and searched related Scriptures to discover a "big truth" about God and His ways. Then she guided the class to consider implications of that truth, thinking through appropriate life responses. This was great—even exhilarating! But the teacher's task was not completed. The only way her pupils can grow spiritually is by actually responding personally to the One who is Truth. And it is at this point that Cheryl sensed she was responsible to have an inner transaction with her God.

She basked in the love of her teacher, the support of her classmates, the spiritual warmth of the class sessions, and in her growing knowledge of God's Word. But it wasn't enough. The lesson wasn't hers until she made her faith-response to the Lord—until she let Him show her what He wanted her to do.

Jesus taught for personal response to Himself. His call was to an "active response" relationship with Himself which motivated daily acts of obedience to His word. He taught obedience both to the God of the Word as well as to the Word of God.

Notice how inner faith responses to His Person and practical, life-changing obedience go hand in hand. Jesus said the wise man who builds his house on a rock rather than on shifting sand, is the one who hears Christ's word and does it (Matt. 7:24). "Come unto Me" (11:28). He invites us to learn *of* Him, not merely about Him. "Go sell your possessions. . . . Then come, follow Me" (19:21, NIV). "Go. . . . And surely I will be with you always" (28:19-20, NIV). "My mother and brothers are those who hear God's Word and put it into practice" (Luke 8:21, NIV). "My sheep listen to My voice. I know them, and they follow Me" (John 10:27 NIV). "Whoever has My commands and obeys them, he is the one who loves Me. He who loves Me will be loved by My Father, and I too will love him and show Myself to him. . . . If anyone loves Me, he will obey My teaching. My Father will love him, and We will come to him and make Our home with him" (14:21, 23, NIV).

Teaching for response

How can you teach for a personal response to Christ? Every sincere teacher asks this. God gives us a satisfying answer—it is His work. He does what a human teacher can never do. He speaks, reproves, woos, wins, converts, reveals truth, transforms lives. But He has chosen to use *you* as a vital part of the process. This is your privilege, a wonderfully high calling. As you do your part, you can depend on Him to do His.

So what is your part? Let's explore some possibilities.

You can be the kind of teacher to whom God speaks.　As you teach, your whole personality reflects your attitude toward the Bible.

Is it your supreme Authority, your Final Court of Appeal in every question of life? Does our living God reveal Himself and His ways to you through its pages? Does your lesson preparation lead you to new encounters with Christ? Your students will know. There's no faking it, and there are no shortcuts. Those who want God to speak to them must also want to live in the Word.

You can be a disciple. Have you ever had a teacher who seemed to have everything down so pat that he didn't want to learn anything more and didn't feel a need for growth? Was it easy to learn from him? A teacher's enthusiasm for growing in Christ is contagious. "I'm a disciple," this kind of teacher says. "I'm learning from Christ every day. Nothing's boring anymore. Even in mundane affairs of living I find opportunities to trust Him and obey His Word. It's the most thrilling challenge of my life!" As you share your feelings about living in a response relationship with Christ, you'll find students longing for the same.

You can provide a climate in which responding to Christ is natural. When you recognize Him as a living Person who is really there in your class, you'll teach with a spirit of expectancy. *He's here!* You'll be relaxed. (I've done my part in faithful, prayerful preparation. Now I'm trusting Christ to teach through me. He'll guide the schedule and show me how to make the best use of time and lesson content.) You'll be approachable. (Christ in me is reaching out to students, accepting them as they are.) You'll be controlled, even when the unexpected occurs. (He's in charge.) You'll have insights to speak to the real person under the surface, not simply addressing yourself to his external behavior. (Christ understands that pupil; He will guide me.) You'll be patient, encouraging each step of faith however small and rejoicing when one is made. This kind of teaching involves not only a prepared lesson but also a prepared life!

Boys and girls open up in an atmosphere where it's safe to reveal inner thoughts and feelings. In one class boys were reporting on their personal Bible reading for the past month. Some gave testimonies of spiritual insights and growth. David spoke up, "I'm glad we're starting a new month. I bombed out on my reading last month. I'm glad God is giving me another chance." Several others in the class nodded their heads sympathetically.

Because you know and love your pupils you will be aware of ways each can respond to the Lord. First, of course, you'll be praying that each will trust Jesus Christ for salvation. You'll be sensitive to the Holy Spirit's leading to enlarge on salvation truths as you teach, to invite interested students to stay after class for private conversation. You'll pray and plan and work, trusting the Holy Spirit to do what He has promised.

Then, because you know children's natural enthusiasm for putting truth into action, you'll trust God to cause them to respond with positive, joy-filled service for God and man. They're becoming mature enough to grasp that stewardship involves all of life— commitment of talents, skills, gifts, time, money, ambitions, friendships, loyalties—all to Christ. As students grow in understanding of God, insight by insight, they can respond by faith in taking small step by small step.

You'll pray for changed attitudes toward God's Word. Personal Bible study can hold a thrill as they turn to the Word in time of need, to depend on their strong, wise God rather than on their own abilities to solve problems.

Children who know the Lord can learn to witness faithfully to their peers by lip and life. Sure, they'll need your practical guidance and Bible instruction, but their response in witnessing will be an outgrowth of their love for Christ.

You can give opportunities to respond. Let's eavesdrop on some teachers.

"Would you like to stay for a minute after class to talk about it?"

"Can you go out for a hamburger with me tomorrow night?"

"Let's each write on a slip of paper how we feel about this week's lesson."

"Can we talk to God as we sing *How Great Thou Art?*"

"Who would like to meet with me on Saturday morning to work on a service project?"

"Use the next moments of silence to tell the Lord how you feel."

What is each teacher doing? Giving his pupils the opportunity to open their lives and respond to the Lord with their teacher at hand to provide loving, prayerful support.

You can encourage sharing. "My lessons don't smack of

reality!" Ellen Walker felt desperate enough to unburden her heart at staff meeting. "I can teach about prayer, but my pupils don't know anyone who is seeing prayer answered. I teach about obedience, but my Juniors don't know anyone who is obeying God when it's hard. I teach about trusting God to meet needs, but they don't know anyone who even admits to having a need." Ellen went on to name other lesson themes.

The other teachers agreed with her that Middlers and Juniors must *see* that Bible truths are real. They need to talk with people who are currently experiencing the reality of living in a faith-response relationship with Christ. Ellen was the obvious one to provide opportunities for this kind of dialogue. She could share herself—some of her own adventures in living responsively with Christ. In addition, teens in the church who were not ready to teach could visit the department to relate briefly some of their experiences of responding to the Lord. Take-home papers that demonstrate God's power in action and biographies of Christians could also help. But one of the most dynamic proofs of the reality of living responsively with Christ was already in Ellen's classroom—her pupils! If she would let them share she would be amazed at how they could help one another!

"Well, aren't you going to ask what happened?" Linda, usually a cooperative child, interrupted her teacher as she got into the week's lesson. Linda—turning into a discipline problem? Hardly! She just couldn't hold it in a moment longer.

"What do you mean?" her teacher asked.

"Last week we each asked the Lord to help us do something that we couldn't do by ourselves. I asked Him to help me not yell at the kids my mom baby-sits. And I think you should all know that He did! I used to be mad that they take my mother's attention when I come home and want to talk about what happened at school. But this week God even helped me play with those little kids!"

You can trust God to do His work. The seed of God's Word, planted in the fertile soil of Linda's heart, had sprung up and borne fruit—so quickly, so miraculously! How her testimony rejoiced the heart of her gardener-teacher. But the same seed had been planted in seven other hearts that previous Sunday. The same gardener-teacher had watered with earnest prayer and warmed with genuine love. Why didn't those seven students bear fruit also?

Here the gardener-teacher remembers God's promise to do His work. Soil conditions vary. In spiritual gardening it takes time to build trust relationships. And, of course, God has not promised that we will always know the results of our faithful seed-planting. We leave those results to Him, knowing that we can trust Him to do all that He has promised to do in the hearts of our students.

The Apostle Paul's prayer is fitting for gardener-teachers. "May the God of hope fill you with great joy and peace as you trust in Him, so that you may overflow with hope by the power of the Holy Spirit" (Rom. 15:13, niv).

Thinking it through

1. Think of a lesson you taught recently. Ask yourself, If my students forgot the factual details of that lesson, what would they retain? Jot down the concepts and life-response that was a part of your lesson.

2. Why is teaching for response so important in Bible instruction?

3. Where are students in your Sunday School seeing that Bible truths are real?

4. Write a prayer about your class from yourself as a gardener-teacher for the Lord, the Master-Gardener.

8
Total-Hour Teaching: Getting It All Together

"Hi, Mr. Bartel. Look at what I made." Sheri holds out a comic strip-type picture series she made at home to tell how she witnessed to a friend.

"Why, Sheri, that's fine. It just fits our theme this month. Let's mount it on the wall so that all of us can enjoy it."

Across the room Mrs. Bartel is talking with Peter, the department memory champion. He has come early to recite a memory passage correlated with the unit theme of witnessing.

As other students arrive, they greet their teachers and choose an early-time activity. Some work on a colorful share-your-faith bulletin board. Others practice reading Scripture for the worship service or form teams to role-play witnessing opportunities. Several become engrossed in a memory verse review game.

Not all students are so motivated, however. Three boys arrive arguing about the world high jump record. Two girls are exchanging favorite books. Another has come without breakfast and is feeling at odds with herself. Teachers spot their reluctant pupils and engage them in friendly conversation.

Then Brad skids through the door. He has more energy than he can handle today. Let's follow him throughout the hour. If his teacher can arouse his want-to—well, that would be something! "Brad," Mr. Clarkson calls, "you're just in time to help us. Would you put this word card at the top of our board?"

Soft piano music calls teachers and children to chairs arranged in semicircles. Brad ducks into a back seat and digs into his pocket for something. Today it's a fake spider. When Mr. Clarkson takes the seat beside him, Brad slips the spider back into his pocket.

Several pupils call the group to worship by reading Scripture reverently. Through song and prayer children join hearts in praising God for His love and asking for love enough to tell others about Christ. A true story, tape-recorded with dialogue, holds attention. It's about Ruth, a 10-year-old who had the joy of helping her friend Diane receive Jesus Christ as Saviour.

Mr. Bartel guides a brief meditation with thought questions: What if Ruth had felt Diane might not like her if she talked about Jesus? What if Ruth had become discouraged when Diane didn't seem interested? What if Ruth and her family had not prayed? It takes something to do what Ruth did—real love for the Lord!

The group expresses concern that people hear about Jesus as they sing sincerely "Who Will Tell Them?" Then, because the boys and girls are genuinely worshiping, they are ready to affirm their desire to witness. Rephrasing Acts 1:8, they read, "Lord, we will be witnesses unto You—to our families, to neighbors and friends, to people who are different, to all who need Christ."

The children go thoughtfully to their classes—except Brad. He takes the long way around and slides into his chair at the last minute, spider cushioned in his warm hand. Mr. Clarkson gives him a good-natured grin that tells Brad, "I'm glad you made it!"

Throughout presession and worship the boys have been thinking about witnessing. Now Mr. Clarkson sharpens the focus to the specific purpose of the lesson: That we may learn ways to communicate basic salvation truths, and be ready to use them.

He chooses two boys to read a brief skit. An early believer has escaped persecution in Jerusalem and is witnessing to a friend in whose home he has found shelter. Brad gets so caught up with the suspense that he provides a few well-timed sound effects! The skit brings the class back to the point where last week's lesson on Stephen's martyrdom left off. It also raises the question, What does God want us to tell others about Jesus' death and resurrection?

Discovering the answer from God's Word follows naturally as Mr. Clarkson tells the thrilling account of Philip witnessing to the

Ethiopian. After listening to the story the boys are ready for a change of pace. They work in their Student Manuals, checking Acts, chapter 8 to do assignments about Philip's witness. Today Mr. Clarkson assigns his boys to work in pairs, putting a more mature pupil with Brad.

Then the boys discuss questions and draw principles, summarized in a colorful visual, for their own witnessing. How did Philip get started witnessing? Why would God take Philip from a big work to witness to just one person? What do you think Philip said about Jesus?

In answering this question one boy takes the part of Philip and Brad speaks for the Ethiopian. It's not simply a replay of the Bible story but reinforces truths Philip communicated as he depended on the Holy Spirit. This role play helps the class discover that they too can witness. And there's an unusual seriousness about Brad as he identifies with the Ethiopian's awareness of need.

"What is important to include in our witness today?" Mr. Clarkson asks. This sends the boys to their Bibles. They read Scripture on their need for salvation, results of sin, the price Jesus paid to save them, and God's promise of eternal life to those who receive His Son.

"It's all here," one boy says in surprise. "All the verses I need to tell that guy who rides the school bus with me."

Mr. Clarkson has prayerfully guided the boys to make their discovery—they have heard how one early Christian witnessed; they have found important truths in Scripture needed for witnessing; and they have put these truths in their own words.

Now they are ready to respond to the Lord. "Are you ready to tell someone about Jesus?" Mr. Clarkson asks. He stresses the truth of the memory verse, Acts 4:20: If we really love the Lord we can't help but talk about Him.

The prayer at the conclusion of the lesson is personal. Each pupil who is ready to do so expresses his love for Jesus, eagerness to tell someone, and asks for help in doing it this week.

Several are ready. And their take-home paper has stories, assignments, and Bible readings that will encourage them to follow through on their decision to witness for Christ.

But Brad? He can't witness because he has not yet received Christ as his Saviour. Discoveries made in this lesson have helped him understand his own need better. And he feels God's love in Mr. Clarkson's friendly understanding. Maybe if Mr. Clarkson talks with him alone after class—maybe the Lord will answer his faithful prayers—maybe this week Brad will say yes!

"Oh," you say, "I wish I could have a class like that!" Mr. Clarkson would assure you that *you can.* Then, with a twinkle in his eye, he would turn from you to call Brad back. "Say, Brad, you forgot your spider!"

Thinking it through

Total hour teaching means simply that all elements in the Sunday School hour are related, each helping accomplish the lesson aim. Examine the Sunday School hour described in this chapter to answer these questions:

1. What was the aim of the lesson?

2. How did teachers use early-time to start students thinking about the lesson theme?

3. How did the department superintendent prepare students for the lesson by his choice of songs, Scripture, true story, and discussion in the worship service?

4. How did Mr. Clarkson's brief skit help his class focus on a significant, aim-related question?

5. List ways Mr. Clarkson involved his boys in discovering God's answer.

6. How did Mr. Clarkson lead his boys to make personal responses?

Additional Resources

Allstrom, Elizabeth. *You Can Teach Creatively*. Nashville, Tenn.: Abingdon Press, 1970.

Barrett, Ethel. *Storytelling—It's Easy*. Grand Rapids, Mich.: Zondervan Publishing House, 1960.

Cohen, Dorothy H. *The Learning Child*. New York: Pantheon Books, 1972.

Dobson, James. *Dare to Discipline*. Wheaton, Ill.: Tyndale House Publishers, 1970.

Edge, Findley B. *Teaching for Results*. Nashville, Tenn.: Broadman Press, 1956.

_____. *Helping the Teacher*. Nashville, Tenn.: Broadman Press, 1959.

Gangel, Kenneth. *24 Ways to Improve Your Teaching*. Wheaton, Ill.: Victor Books, 1974.

Getz, Gene A. *Audio Visuals in the Church*. Chicago, Ill.: Moody Press, 1960.

Joy, Donald M. *Meaningful Learning in the Church*. Winona Lake, Ind.: Light and Life Press, 1969.

LeBar, Lois E. *Children in the Bible School*. Westwood, N.J.: Fleming H. Revell Company, 1952.

_____. *Education that Is Christian*. Westwood, N.J.: Fleming H. Revell Company, 1958.

LeBar, Mary E. *Children Can Worship*. Wheaton, Ill.: Victor Books, 1976.

McDaniel, Elsiebeth and Richards, Lawrence O. *You and Children*. Chicago, Ill.: Moody Press, 1973.

Morningstar, Mildred. *Reaching Children*. Chicago, Ill.: Moody Press, 1944.

Morrison, Eleanor Shelton and Foster, Virgil E. *Creative Teaching in the Church*. Englewood Cliffs, N.J.: Prentice Hall, Inc., 1963.

Mow, Anna B. *Your Child—From Birth to Rebirth*. Grand Rapids, Mich.: Zondervan Publishing House, 1963.

Richards, Lawrence O. *You the Teacher*. Chicago, Ill.: Moody Press, 1972.

Soderholm, Marjorie. *Explaining Salvation to Children*. Minneapolis, Minn.: Free Church Publications, 1962.

_____. *Salvation . . . Then What?* Minneapolis, Minn.: Free Church Publications, 1968.

_____. *The Junior*. Grand Rapids, Mich.: Baker Book House, 1956.

Zuck, Roy B. *Spiritual Power in Your Teaching*. Chicago, Ill.: Moody Press, 1972.

Zuck, Roy B. and Clark, Robert E., Editors. *Childhood Education in the Church*. Chicago, Ill.: Moody Press, 1975.